For Steve, Teresa, Stephanie, Rebekah, and Jessica
— R.G.G.

To all my inspiring friends
— A.W.

Text © 2002 Rhonda Gowler Greene
Illustrations © 2002 Anne Wilson

Published 2002 by Eerdmans Books for Young Readers
An imprint of Wm. B. Eerdmans Publishing Company
255 Jefferson S.E., Grand Rapids, Michigan 49503
P.O. Box 163, Cambridge CB3 9PU U.K.

Library of Congress-in-Publication Data
Greene, Rhonda Gowler.
The Beautiful World That God Made / written by Rhonda Gowler Greene;
illustrated by Anne Wilson. p. cm.
Summary: A retelling of the Creation story, in which various
features of the Earth and its inhabitants are praised for their
beauty, splendor, and role in the beginning of the world.

ISBN 0-8028-5213-0 (alk. paper)
1. Creation-Juvenile literature. [1. Creation.]
I. Wilson, Anne ill. II. Title.
BT695.G718 2002
231.7'65—dc21   2001040175

The illustrations were rendered in printing inks and collaged papers.
The display type was set in Countryhouse.
The text type was set in Futura.
Designed by Jesi Josten.

The Beautiful World that God Made

Written by
Rhonda Gowler Greene

Illustrated by
Anne Wilson

Eerdmans Books for Young Readers
Grand Rapids, Michigan • Cambridge, U.K.

This is the beautiful world that God made.

This is the light,

brilliant and bright,

that formed the first day

from a dark, endless night

and started the beautiful world

that God made.

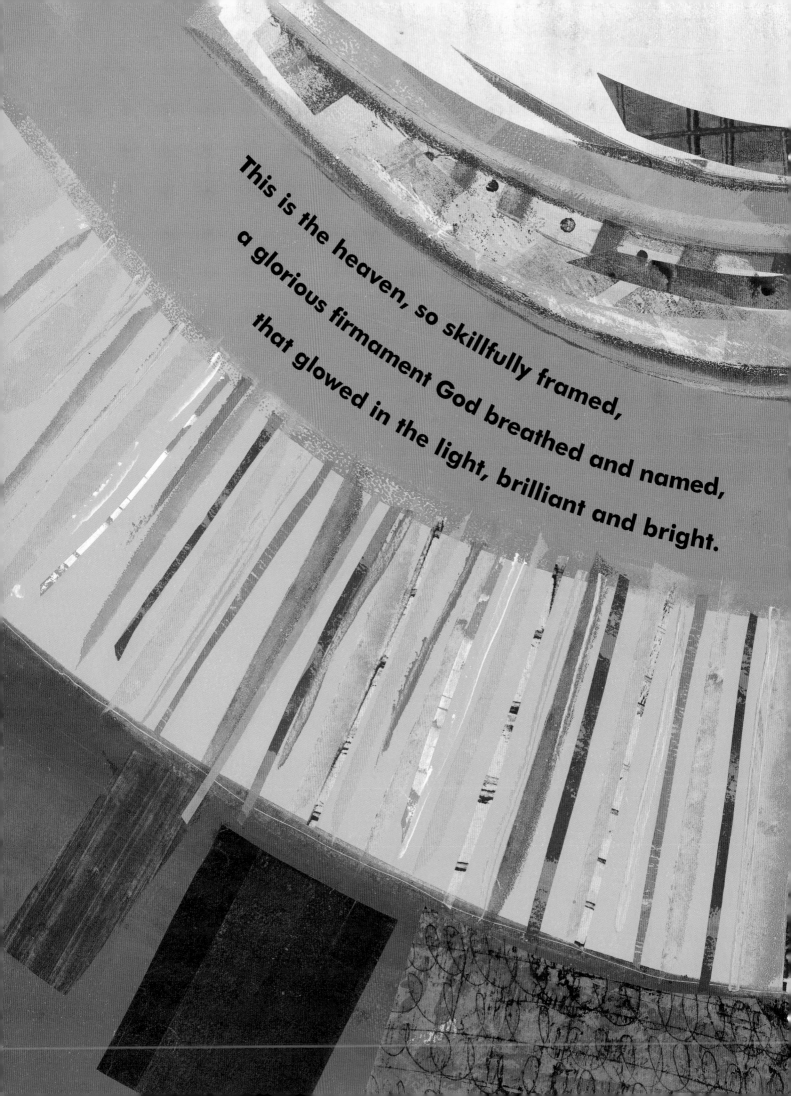

This is the heaven, so skillfully framed,
a glorious firmament God breathed and named,
that glowed in the light, brilliant and bright.

This is the land and God-gathered seas,
the grass, ferns and flowers, the fruit-bearing trees,
that sat beneath heaven, so skillfully framed.

These are the stars, the moon, and the sun,
the circle of seasons cleverly spun
enfolding the land and God-gathered seas.

These are the creatures all in his plan,

two in his image — woman and man,

that walked near the fish and fowl of the air.

This is the day God chose to rest, to look on the world he created and blessed,

and delight in the creatures all in his plan,

two in his image — woman and man,

that walked near the fish and fowl of the air

that multiplied quickly, sprang forth everywhere,

under the stars, the moon, and the sun,
the circle of seasons cleverly spun

enfolding the land and God-gathered seas,

the grass, ferns and flowers, the fruit-bearing trees

that sat beneath heaven, so skillfully framed,

a glorious firmament God breathed and named

that glowed in the light,

brilliant and bright,

that formed the first day

from a dark, endless night

and started the beautiful world that God made.